DO-IT-YOURSELF FRAMING

Yes, you can frame your own pictures using tools and supplies readily available from art supply, photography, or craft supply stores. Photographs, paintings, art prints, children's art, diplomas, newspaper clippings, and needlework are just a few of the many items the do-it-yourself framer can frame for display.

Picture framing is an important part of room decor. It allows us to display photographs of favorite people and places. It lets treasured memorabilia be part of daily life, instead of tucked away in a drawer. Framed items and images can express personal interests, or celebrate special events. They can define and coordinate decorating schemes, highlighting or introducing favorite colors.

Picture framing requires a variety of skills, and a working knowledge of materials and equipment. But with a little practice and the right tools, a handy craftsperson can learn to produce attractive and well-crafted framed pieces at home.

People are often interested in framing their own pieces because they enjoy the craft of framing, or because they want an economical means of framing. This book is a guide to accomplishing those goals. The most important skills required are a good eye, a steady hand and a willingness to learn.

THE PURPOSE OF FRAMING

Picture framing provides two important services for a piece of art—protection and presentation.

Protection is provided with proper materials and methods. Presentation begins with designing the project. The presentation should complement the art. "Overdoing" is a tendency of amateurs in any field of endeavor, and sometimes the beginner framer "over frames" the piece both visually and structurally. In an attempt to make it look professional, the art is sometimes overwhelmed by the framing. The goal is a presentation that allows a viewer to see the beauty of the artwork and not be distracted by the framing.

Professional picture framers learn their skills and techniques through years of apprenticeship, training, and trial and error. The methods suggested here are designed to expedite the learning process, allowing home framers to begin framing right away, while giving a "professional" finish to the work.

The mechanics of framing are important, but equally important are the aesthetics of framing—the style, color, and proportion of the frame and matting. Understanding these elements makes all the difference between a "homemade" and a professional-looking presentation.

A NOTE ABOUT CONSERVATION FRAMING

Professional picture framers use the term "conservation" to refer to the materials and techniques used for framing art of value, whether that value is sentimental or monetary. The goal is preservation, protecting the art and ensuring that the framing process itself does no harm.

For conservation framing, all materials must be clean, stable, and acid-free, and all materials in contact with the art must be completely reversible without any damage to the art.

In this book, conservation measures are suggested or described where applicable. The basic materials required are available at many art supply or craft supply stores.

Fine art should be framed using fine quality materials and conservation procedures.

Treasured family photographs can be preserved using the proper materials and methods.

DO-IT-YOURSELF
PICTURE FRAMING

Do-It-Yourself Picture Framing
by Vivian Kistler, Certified Picture Framer, USA
    Guild Commended Framer, UK

© 2001 Logan Graphic Products, Inc. Wauconda, Illinois

All International Rights Reserved
First Edition
Printed in the United States of America
Published by Columba Publishing Co., Inc.
Akron, Ohio

ISBN 0-938655-88-4

10 9 8 7 6 5 4 3 2

Please request permission or further information from the Permissions Department, Columba Publishing Company, 2003 W. Market St., Akron, Ohio 44313. USA Telephone: 1.330.836.2619 Fax: 1.330.836.9659.

ART & PHOTOGRAPHY CREDITS

Cathy Welner, watercolors page 10, page 56
Luciano Duse, photograph page 16
Barbara Schlueter, photograph top page 60
Alice Marvin, ink sketches page 19, page 58
Laine Kistler, painting page 5, page page 62LR
Carli Kistler, crewel work page 5
Sheri Galat, ribbon work page 29
Patricia Jolly, photograph page 59L
Richmond, acrylic painting page 62 center
Vivian Kistler, encaustic, page 62 top
T. Leighton, pastel drawing page 6

PHOTOGRAPHERS:
Andy Fiala 6, 10, 14, 18, 23, 43
Barbara Schlueter 16LL, 27, 34, 38, 41, 55, 58L
Heather Protz 5, 7, 8, 11, 13, 16, 17, 28, 29, 31, 37, 39, 44, 45, 53, 54, 56, 57, 58, 59, 60, 61, 62

ILLUSTRATORS:
Marla Strasburg Crawford
Kelly Ross

ART REPRODUCTIONS:
    Wild Apple Graphics 13, 14, 16, 28, 54T
    Main Floor Editions 37
    Arts Unique 5, 27

CONTENTS

FRAMES

Perhaps the easiest way to frame pictures yourself is to use ready-made frames and make mats to fit the frame and the art. Frames are available in a wide variety of shapes, styles, finishes and materials. Frames are sold in art supply, photography, hobby and craft supply stores as well as some department and discount stores, and, of course, in picture framing shops.

When choosing a frame, the style and strength is important. The frame must be strong enough to bear the weight of all the materials it will hold. Glass is heavy, so a large piece of artwork that will be glassed requires a strong frame.

SIZE

The lip and inner sides of the frame, which accommodate the framing materials, is called the "rabbet," and the inside frame measurement is called the "rabbet size." Make sure there is room for all of the layers that are planned. The glass, matboards, artwork, and backing board must fit into the frame without bulging out of the back.

A frame that is said to measure 16"x20" has a rabbet size of 16-1/8" x 20-1/8". This allows a bit of expansion space for materials which are cut to 16"x20".

Ready-made frames are available in a wide selection from art, craft and hobby dealers.

READY-MADE FRAMES

Frames are available in standard sizes. They may be made from many types of wood, expanded plastic, molded plastics, composition material or aluminum. There is a wide variety of colors and styles in standard sizes. Ready-made frames may be sold empty or packaged with matting and glass.

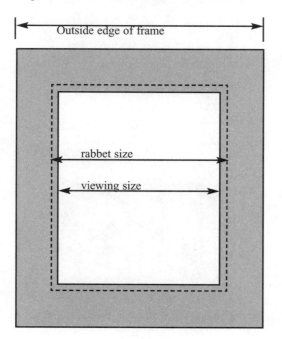

A list of the standard sizes found in the art, craft, photography and picture framing industry:

4x5	**11x14**	**24x36**
4x6	12x16	26x32
5x7	14x18	30x40
6x8	**16x20**	**32x40**
8x10	18x24	36x48
8x12	**20x24**	40x60
8-1/2x11	22x28	48x60
9x12	**24x30**	48x96

Although ready-made frames and mats are available in many sizes, the sizes printed in bold are the most common.

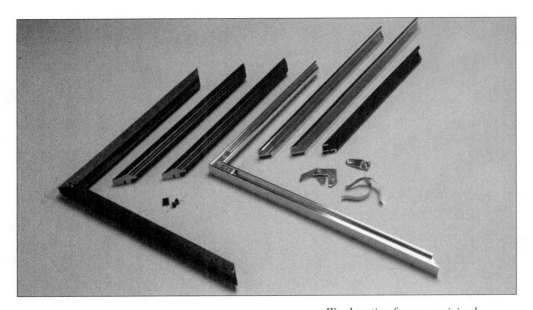

SECTION FRAMES

Section frames are sold in pairs; two pairs make a frame. Several types of wood frames and metal frames are available in sections. The pairs of sections allow endless size options for the custom-made look for each frame project.

Each wood frame rail has a section routed out in each corner to hold a plastic wedge that will hold the corners together.

Metal frames are made from extruded aluminum. The typical style is about 3/4" deep, with a narrow, flat front. Typical options are a shiny chrome or brass finish, and perhaps black. The corners are joined with metal L-shaped brackets or plastic inserts. Hangers are normally provided with the hardware.

PHOTO FRAMES

Ready-made "photo frames," which typically come equipped with glass, backing and easel backs typically accommodate only a photograph and one mat.

Wood section frames are joined using glue and wedges. Metal section frames are joined using metal corner brackets.

Plastic wedges are inserted in the routed-out area on the back side of the moulding. They, along with glue, hold the mitered corners of a wood section frame.

This snapshot is framed using a ready-made 5x7 photo frame combined with a ready-made double mat.

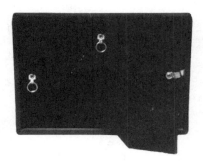

Photo frames often have both hangers and an easel back.

PLASTIC BOX FRAMES

Box frames are made of clear plastic, pre-formed to standard sizes, generally between 5" x 7" and 16" x 20". The box usually consists of two pieces, a cardboard box and a clear plastic "cap" that fits snugly over the cardboard. The snug fit allows for only one mat, at the most. The box usually has holes on the back side, for hanging on the head of a nail.

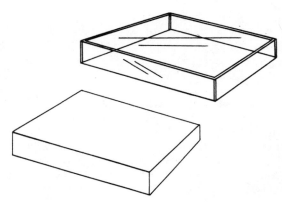

QUICK FRAMES

There are a number of styles of "quick frames," various systems of metal or plastic clips or strips that are either self-contained or joined with a wire or cord. These are not full frames, because they do not enclose the perimeter of the artwork. They simply attach to the artwork at the corners and/or sides, holding the layers (glass, mat, art, backing) together and providing a temporary hanging system. These frames have size limitations.

This type of framing is considered temporary because dust, air pollution and moisture can easily invade the framing package.

Most quick frames involve a channel in a clip or strip which must be filled—but not too tightly. If the framing materials do not fill the channel, add more backing board. The sharp edges of the surface glass are exposed in these frames, but the edges can be ground smooth at a glass shop or in the home workshop with an oilstone from the hardware store.

Most quick frames require either glass or backing or both for the necessary rigidity.

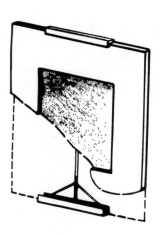

Top and bottom plastic channels are held together with cord.

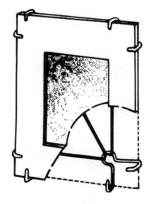

Metal corner clips are held together with cord.

BOARDS FOR FRAMING

In picture framing, the term "board" generally refers to various types of paper board sheets. Boards are used for matting, backing, mounting, and filler. They are made especially for picture framing.

There are acids in many papers and boards, especially those made from wood pulp. Acids can cause paper and boards to turn yellow and deteriorate (think of an old newspaper), and can cause the same sort of damage to the artwork they come in contact with. Many paper products are "buffered" with calcium carbonate or other chemicals during production to neutralize these acids. Such products are then labeled "acid-free." Buffering is very effective, but may not last forever.

Boards are like fine art papers, they are made from chemically processed wood pulp or pure cotton. Cotton is naturally white and acid-free, and therefore requires far less bleaching and processing during manufacturing. The finest papers and boards for art and framing are made from cotton. Most watercolor papers and printmaking papers are made from cotton. Mat or mount boards that are made from cotton are often called "Rag," from an old papermaker's term referring to the strips of cotton scrap used in the papermaking process.

DO NOT USE
Brown corrugated board, poster board, construction paper, and shirt cardboard are unsuitable for framing purposes.

MATTING
Matting is a border that surrounds and supports artwork. Matboard is designed especially for picture framing. Most matboards consist of a surface sheet that carries the color and texture of the board, a backing sheet, and several tightly compressed layers that make up the core. Matboard is available in many colors and a number of textures, including simulated linen, marble, and flannel. Matboards are typically 32" x 40", but some are available 40" x 60". Boards for cutting custom mats are available from art supply and craft stores.

Mats are sometimes called window mats, because they provide a window through which the art is viewed. This fine watercolor is double-matted using cotton rag matboards.

MATBOARDS

STANDARD OR REGULAR MATBOARD: This board is made from processed woodpulp. If the package states it is acid-free, the board has been buffered to neutralize the acids, especially in the wood pulp core. The buffering will help the wood pulp last longer. Many wood pulp boards will discolor and become dry and brittle over time.

CONSERVATION MATBOARD: These boards have either a cotton or purified wood pulp (alpha) core, plus buffered, acid-free surface and backing papers.

RAG MATBOARD: Museum grade matboard. Cotton throughout. Made from cotton pulp compressed into a solid sheet. Highest quality board.

UNSUITABLE BOARDS
POSTER BOARD: This is an acidic craft board, meant for short-term use. Moisture-sensitive, fades and deteriorates rather quickly.

CARDBOARD, CONSTRUCTION PAPER, ETC.: These and similar types of craft materials have high acidity and uneven density that makes them unsuitable.

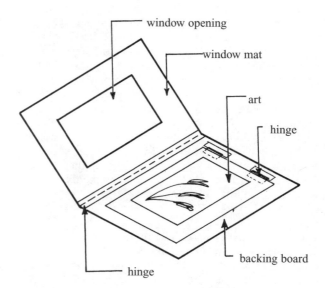

A "mat package" consists of a window mat and a backing board. The backing board is usually made of the same kind of board as the mat. The two boards are often attached to one another with tape, either along the top edge or along the left side.

PRE-CUT MATS
Art supply and craft stores generally carry ready-made mats in a variety of colors in standard sizes. These are quick and convenient for the do-it-yourself framer.

Boards for Backing, Mounting and Filler

Besides matting, boards are also used in picture framing for backing (the board that goes immediately behind the artwork and supports the art), for mounting (bonding the art to the surface of a board), and for filler (extra board that goes into the frame for additional support during final assembly of the framing package.)

When choosing these boards, the decision is based on the quality and sturdiness needed for the artwork. Choose a board that is strong enough, but don't overdo it. Nothing needs to be backed with or mounted to Masonite®—it is very heavy and highly acidic. Corrugated cardboard is lightweight and sturdy, but it is very acidic and its ridges may show through the artwork.

Textured boards are unsuitable for mounting because of this tendency to show through. Poster board is too flimsy. Chipboard is highly acidic and deteriorates over time.

Suitable options for backing, filler, and mounting boards are:

MOUNTING BOARD
These boards have smooth white surfaces made especially for mounting. Available in various thicknesses for different mounting needs. Also available acid-free.

MATBOARD
Primarily for matting and backing, matboard can be used as a filler board and it may be used for most mounting applications. If desired, mount the art on a color that coordinates with the artwork and leave a border of the mat color showing around the art.

FOAM CENTER BOARD
Styrofoam core with smooth surface papers adhered to both sides. Lightweight and sturdy, available in several thicknesses (1/8", 1/4", 1/2"). Strong enough for large artwork. An acid-free version is available for use as conservation mounting or backing board.

ILLUSTRATION BOARD
Although typically used by graphic artists, illustration board may be used as a backing and mounting board.

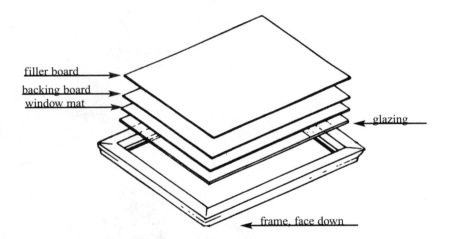

filler board
backing board
window mat
glazing
frame, face down

COLOR & DESIGN

Operating side-by-side with the craft of framing is the artistic aspect. The framing should serve as an attractive presentation for the artwork.

CHOOSING THE FRAME

Picture frames are available in a wide variety of styles and materials. The best choice for each framing project depends on the most suitable presentation for the piece being framed.

Try this exercise: look at the artwork, describe it, then look at the chosen frame. Adjectives such as strong, dark, pale, or soft describe entirely different styles of art as well as styles of frames. Do the same adjectives describe the art and frame? If so, it is probably a good combination.

There is also the "visual weight" to consider. A narrow metal moulding may be strong enough to handle the actual weight of a 30" x 40" oil painting, but may not provide a good presentation for the art, looking out of balance. On the other hand, an 8" x 10" oil painting may only require a narrow, plain frame to manage its physical weight, but may be more beautifully presented in a wide, ornate gold frame.

CHOOSING MAT COLORS

Matting protects the art from touching the glass, and allows air circulation within the frame. The mat has an aesthetic purpose as well. It can highlight a color in the artwork, accent a shape, or simply increase the size, making a more dramatic display for the art.

Let the mat colors complement the character of the art. What colors are in the artwork? In what proportions? Lots of dark green? Just a little blue? What is the mood or feeling of the image depicted? Soft, bright, dark? These are the guidelines to use when choosing the mats.

Often artwork is framed for a specific location in the home, such as over the couch. For these pictures, it is fine to choose mat colors that help coordinate the decorating scheme—but if those colors do not appear in the artwork at least a little bit, it will look like a "forced fit." In those situations, try a double mat with a neutral top mat and a liner mat that accents the room colors.

The wide frame on this small painting gives the art importance, and draws the eye to the art.

Beginners often fear that large mat borders will overwhelm small artwork, but in reality a wide mat border focuses attention on the art and gives it an importance it deserves.

PROPORTION

Proportion is a relationship between various parts of a whole thing. Unless a person is an artist or a scientist, well-balanced visual proportion is something one sees rather than measures. It is a personal visual balance of light, color, texture, shape, and line. The proportions an individual feels most comfortable with are based on a life-time of personal, cultural, and educational (both formal and informal) experiences.

In picture framing, the size of the matting is very impor-tant to the presentation of the art. Beginners typically choose narrow mat borders, thinking that a wider border might overwhelm the art. In fact, the opposite is often true, as narrow borders become stripes that can distract the viewer from focusing on the art.

In museums, very large mats are used, even on small pieces of art, to showcase the art itself. This style is fre-quently adopted when framing fine art for homes and offices. At first, these wide mat borders may look over-sized, but as picture framers gain more experience, they usually start to prefer wider mats.

One traditional matting proportion is a wider bottom bor-der. The top and sides are one size, and the bottom is either slightly wider or may be as much as several inches wider. There are a variety of theories about why this pro-portion is appealing to the human eye, including elements like gravity and natural proportions. For picture framing purposes it is enough to know that a heavier bottom mat border provides a comfortable balance for many viewers. It is commonly used on fine art and photography, and is often seen in museums.

Look at the examples on this page, and notice the differ-ences created by adjusting the width of the borders. Experiment with wider mats, especially in neutral colors.

Mat Styles

Museum Matting
Typically white, black or pale neutral colors. The art is often placed in the upper area leaving a very large lower margin. Often museums use this style when mounting a collection of different size pieces using frames of uniform size. Especially suitable on small images.

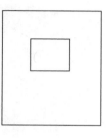

Weighted Bottom Mat
Equal borders on the top and sides, extra width on bottom border. The amount of weight may be slight or moderate, appearing balanced when viewed. Whether rooted in the Victorian tradition

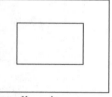

of hanging pictures very high on the wall, or in response to a natural visual preference for a solid base, this style is an attractive design option for both traditional and contemporary art.

Oriental Style Mat
A traditional oriental proportion based on the proportions of paintings done on scrolls. Used both vertically and horizontally depending on the artwork. To mimic scroll proportions, the narrow sides are one third or less than the width of the wider sides.

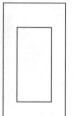

Roman/Gothic Mat
This arched design conveys a feeling of tradition, antiquity, and romance. Suitable on Renaissance prints, wedding, and ancestral photos. For visual balance, a bit less matting is used on the top than on the sides and bottom. The rounded arch is Roman; the pointed is Gothic.

French Matting
This traditional style, also called wash panels, is created with subtle-colored painted panels and a series of ink lines. Frequently used on 19th-century etchings and watercolors, French matting can bring an air of refinement to traditional reproductions as well. For the

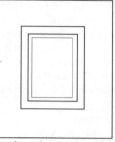

best visual balance, keep the decorative elements within the first third of mat width from the mat opening.

Spandrel Mat
An oval or circle within a rectangle or square is called a spandrel. The curve of a mat opening can give elegance, dignity, and grace to a design. Because oval and circle openings invite central focus they are especially suited to art which is featured in the center such as vignettes, portraits and sketches.

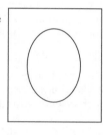

Print Mat
Often this design is used to accommodate the size of the artist's printmaking paper. To preserve the value of original art on paper, the paper should

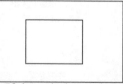

not be cut or altered in any way. If the painting, print, drawing, etc. is done on a large sheet of paper, matting can cover the excess "carrier sheet."

DESIGNING MATS FOR STANDARD SIZE FRAMES

Ready-made frames are available in standard sizes (page 7). All of the standard sizes are based on some practical purpose. For example, 5" x 7", 8" x 10", and 11" x 14", among others, are designed to coordinate with the photography industry. Some of the larger sizes are based on the size of a sheet of watercolor paper, or the most common sizes of stretched canvas.

Unfortunately, the art one chooses to frame doesn't always fit into these standard sizes. The fit may be comfortable vertically, but not horizontally, or perhaps the problem is the other way around.

Look at the drawings at the right, showing art placed in standard-sized frames with various possibilities for apportioning the mat borders. Personal preference is the most important guide for determining which is best.

Color also plays a role in the decision. If the proportions of the mat borders are not quite ideal, a mat color that blends with the art will make the size difference less obvious than a contrasting color.

The number of mats chosen for a piece of art is another decision influenced by the amount of space available. If the mat border will be very wide, using double or triple mats can help to break up the expanse. For a narrow mat border, just one mat is best, to avoid a distracting, striped effect.

A standard size 16"x20" frame and 16"x20" mat with an 11"x14" opening. The mat border is 3" at the top and bottom while the sides are 2-1/2".

5"x7" photograph, custom-cut mat, 12"x16" standard size frame.

Ready-made frame, ready-made double mat. The postcard is attached to a background matboard.

16"x20" frame with an 11"x14" opening ready-made mat.

MAT CUTTERS & ACCESSORIES

Boards used for mats and mounting are dense and require special tools to cut them. Boards will have to be cut down to size, which requires a straight cutter; openings for window mats require a bevel cut which can be achieved with a bevel cutter.

Mat and board cutting tools can be as simple as a straight edge and a knife with a blade, but control and straight lines are difficult. The Team system pictured at the right is a straightedge which provides a track for the bevel cutting head to ride on. This insures a straight cut.

The cutters illustrated here are suitable for cutting well-crafted mats with the beveled edges that are an important feature of fine quality matting.

Whichever cutter is selected, sharp blades and plenty of practice are the keys to success. Do not expect perfection the first time or even the fifth time. Like any new skill or new tool, it takes a little experience to get a "feel" for it.

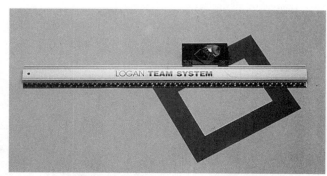

Team System bevel cutting head and straight edge.

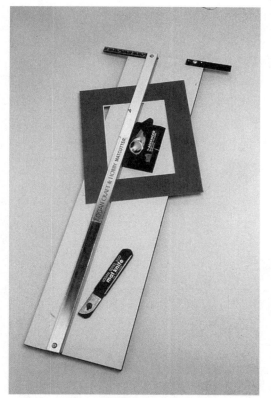

The Logan Craft & Hobby Board Cutter provides a sturdy base, guide rail, bevel cutting head and a straight cutting hand knife.

The Logan Oval Mat & Board Cutter cuts beveled circles and ovals in matboards.

These cutters are available through most art and craft supply stores. They are moderately priced and provide accurate cutting of mat and mounting boards for picture framing and other crafts.

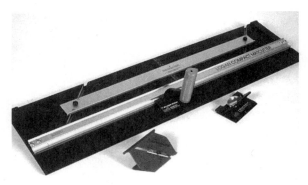

Compact Mat Cutter with bevel head, straight cut head and foam board cutter.

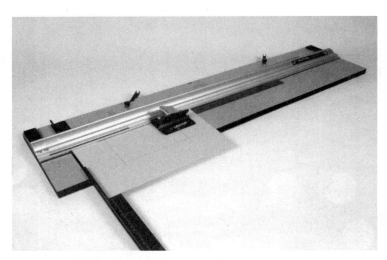

Simplex Mat Cutter #750. Full size cutter with guide rail, bevel cutting head which rides on the guide rail, extension bar for measuring and cutting boards.

GLAZING

The term "glazing" refers to both glass and plastic. Glass can be purchased by the lite (single sheet) or by the box from glass and mirror shops, art supply and craft supply stores, picture framers and hardware stores. Glass can be cut to size at some of these stores, or larger sizes can be bought and cut to size at home.

While glazing provides valuable protection to framed art, it is important to keep the glass away from the surface of the art. Ordinary humidity changes can cause artwork pressed against the glazing to stick to the glazing, and the lack of airspace can promote the formation of mold as moisture gets trapped in the frame. Use mats or other spacers in the framing to lift the glazing from the surface of the art.

REGULAR CLEAR GLASS
This is ordinary window glass. Picture framing glass is thinner, and flawless, although window glass may be used. Regular glass allows clear viewing of framed items at any depth, although there may be problems with glare.

NON-GLARE GLASS
This is clear glass etched or texturized to minimize reflections. Non-glare glass can cause viewing distortion when placed at a distance from artwork or objects.

UV-FILTERING GLASS
Also called conservation glass, this glass filters ultraviolet light rays, which are harmful to art. It is not a complete shield, and even with it, art should still be protected from too much light exposure.

PLASTIC
Plastic is about half the weight of glass, so it is a good choice for large frames or for children's play areas. Do not use plastics on pastels or charcoal drawings because the static of the plastic will lift particles off the art paper.

Acrylic is the best plastic for picture framing. It is sometimes available in standard sizes from frame shops or art supply stores. For other sizes, it can be purchased custom-cut to size from a glass supplier, or large sheets can be purchased and cut as needed. Use a sturdy thickness, such as 1/8". Acrylic usually comes with paper sheeting attached to both sides. Leave this protective paper on as long as possible. Styrene is a cheaper type of plastic; it yellows over time from exposure to heat and light.

Pastels, pencil drawings, watercolors, and pen & inks require glazing to protect the medium and the paper they are created on.

ADHESIVES & ATTACHMENTS

All artwork must be attached to a support board (backing board) before framing. The choice of adhesive or other attachment materials is important to the appearance and longevity of the art.

ATTACHMENTS FOR FLAT ARTWORK

Polyvinyl tapes, such as Scotch Magic Tape are suitable adhesives for the majority of practical framing jobs. Polyvinyl tapes are strong, clean, and stable, but permanent.

Double-stick tapes are useful for various framing attachments, such as attaching mats to one another, and floating decorative art on a matboard.

<u>Do Not Use</u> cellophane, surgical, filament, duct, or masking tape, nor rubber cement. These adhesives first get very sticky, then eventually dry out, leaving deep stains on the artwork. Even for art that is purely decorative, there are much better choices available.

If the artwork is valuable, or may become valuable in the future, use a conservation framing adhesive. These are acid-free, water-reversible adhesives, which can be completely removed without affecting the artwork. The favorite of professionals is wheat or rice starch paste. The adhesive is applied to torn strips of Japanese paper (also called rice paper) to make hinges for attaching artwork to the support board. There are also Japanese papers sold in strips precoated with appropriate paste, ready to apply with water. All of these hinging materials are available in art supply and some craft stores.

Many art supply and craft stores sell gummed tapes that are water reversible, and these are also suitable for conservation attachments. The adhesive comes on a linen or paper support, and is activated by water. Some gummed tapes are too thick for art on thin paper, causing a ridge that shows on the front of the art, but these thick tapes can be useful for hinging heavy artwork, such as watercolors done on thick paper.

The specific attachments and adhesives for mounting procedures, shadow boxes, and needlework are discussed within the sections on those topics.

Each decorative postcard is attached to the matboard backing using a strip of double-stick tape at the top edge of the postcard.

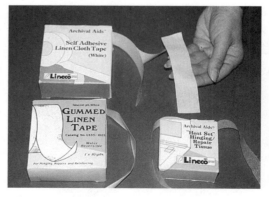

These tapes can be used for conservation hinging.

BASIC FRAMING TECHNIQUES

MEASURING

Accurate measurements are very important in every phase of picture framing. Working with fractions is a part of that accuracy.

Fractions represent parts of an inch. The pictures on this page offer a simple explanation of the most typical fractions.

MEASURING FRAMES

Measuring the face of a frame reveals how much space it will need on a wall, but for framing purposes, frames are measured from the back inside edge of the frame—the rabbet. This is the space that will accommodate the glass, artwork, and boards. When framing, the rabbet size is a crucial measurement.

The rabbet size of a frame should be slightly larger than the glass, mats, and backing boards, to provide a comfortable fit and allow for expansion and contraction of materials during changes in heat and humidity. A so-called 8" x 10" frame typically measures 8-1/8" x 10-1/8" when measured tightly inside the rabbet. The materials that go into the frame must be cut slightly smaller (8" x 10").

Example:
1. The vertical photo measures 7-1/4" x 9-1/4".

2. After adding the mat (the window mat opening measures 7" x 9", and there are 3" of matting on each of the four sides) the matted picture measures 13" x 15".

3. Matboards, glass, and backing will be cut to 13" x 15".

4. The exact rabbet size of the frame will be 13-1/8" x 15-1/8".

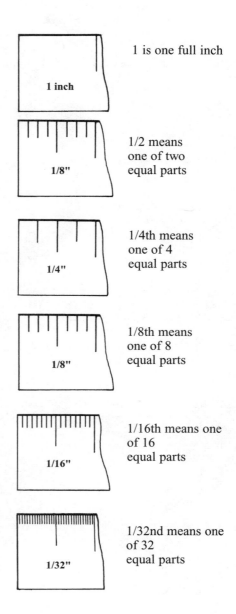

1 inch — 1 is one full inch

1/8" — 1/2 means one of two equal parts

1/4" — 1/4th means one of 4 equal parts

1/8" — 1/8th means one of 8 equal parts

1/16" — 1/16th means one of 16 equal parts

1/32" — 1/32nd means one of 32 equal parts

MAT MATHEMATICS

To determine the opening of the mat, measure the artwork. The mat must cover at least 1/8" of the artwork on all sides, in order to prevent the edges from peeking through or actually falling through the mat opening.

After the proper opening is established, add the amount of matting desired.

1. Add the amount of both side borders to the horizontal opening measurement.
2. Add the width of both the top and bottom borders to the vertical opening measurement.

It is often useful to add extra matting to the border size so the measurements become round numbers which are easier to work with. For example:

An 8" x 10" photograph has an actual opening of 7-3/4" x 9-3/4". With a 2" mat border on all four sides, the outside mat edge will be 11-3/4" x 13-3/4".

By adding an 1/8" to each border (now 2-1/8"), the result is a 12" x 14" mat, which will also be the size of the frame and glass.

This will be true for almost every mat that is cut. Consequently, when a mat opening is 8" x 10", it is probably 7-3/4" x 9-3/4", if not 7-1/2" x 9-1/2". Always check the exact image size and where the opening will be positioned on the artwork.

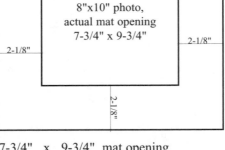

8"x10" photo, actual mat opening 7-3/4" x 9-3/4"

2-1/8"

7-3/4" x 9-3/4" mat opening
4-1/4" x 4-1/4" (two borders)
12"   x 14"   mat, glass & frame size

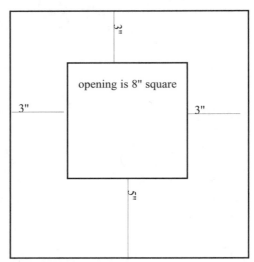

opening is 8" square

3"

5"

8" x 8" mat opening
3"   3" side borders
3"   5" top and bottom borders
14" x 16" mat, glass & frame size

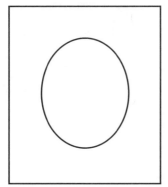

5"   x   7"   mat opening
1-1/2"   1-1/2" side borders
1-1/2"   1-1/2" top and bottom borders
8"   x   10" mat, glass & frame size

TRIMMING A BOARD TO SIZE & SLIP SHEETS

In picture framing, trimming a board to the size needed for matting or backing is called "blanking" the board. Board pieces need to be cut as accurately as possible, paying attention to both size and squareness. Squared corners and straight sides are especially important when blanking boards for mats, because flaws in these boards will result in very obvious problems with the squareness of the mat opening.

Blanking can be done using a straight line or hand-held mat cutter, an X-Acto® knife or utility blade guided by a t-square, or a guillotine-style paper cutter (if the blade is strong enough to handle the board.)

SLIP SHEETS

A slip sheet is a strip of matboard that rests beneath a blanked board while a mat is being cut. During the mat cutting, the cutter blade slices all the way through the matboard that will become the mat, and cuts just slightly into the slip sheet. This helps control the cut, provides cleaner cuts, and helps make the corner intersections neat and square. Without a slip sheet, ragged cuts and "hooked" corners can be a problem.

Slip sheets are typically between 5"-10" wide, and at least several inches longer than the mat being cut. If using a mat cutter that has its own baseboard, the ideal length for the slip sheet is at least 2/3 the length of the baseboard. Matboard for slip sheets is usually readily available from the scrap board left over after blanking boards for mats.

Use a hand-held straight cutter to trim matboards to size. The cutter can be used with a T-square or in conjunction with several mat cutters.

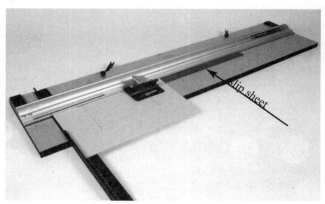

Using a slip sheet provides cleaner cuts.

MAT CUTTING

No matter what kind of equipment is used for cutting mats, certain principles apply.

- The base of the mat cutter must be fully supported and level.
- Use a good T-square (no wobble in the head) when measuring.
- Use a slip sheet (a narrow scrap of matboard) on the face of the cutting board.
- Set the depth of the cutter blade so that it slices through the matboard and slightly scratches the slip sheet.
- Always use sharp blades. It is cheaper to throw away pennies for a new blade than dollars for a new matboard.
- Slide the blade smoothly into the matboard. Do not poke or jab.
- Keep matboards in a dry place. Moisture makes boards difficult to cut.
- Always use pencil to mark the mat borders for cutting. Never use marker or pen, which can seep into the matboard or smear.

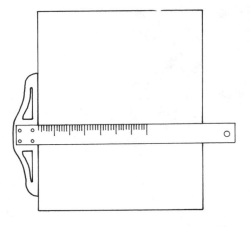

CUTTING A SINGLE MAT USING A HAND-HELD CUTTER

1. Trim the matboard to size.

2. With a T-square and pencil, measure and mark the mat borders desired on the back side of the matboard.

3. Place the mat face down on a piece of board that is larger than the matboard being cut.

4. Set the T-square on the penciled line. Lean on the head of the T-square to keep it in position.

5. Set the cutter against the T-square. Insert the cutting blade, lining up the placement marking on the cutter with the pencil line.

6. Push or pull the blade, depending on the type of cutter being used, until the placement marking on the cutter reaches the next pencil line.

7. Cut all four sides in this manner, stopping and starting carefully.

Logan #1100 push style
hand-held cutter

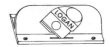

Logan #2000 push style
hand-held cutter

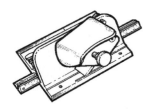

Logan #4000 pull style
hand-held cutter

CUTTING A SINGLE MAT
WITH A STRAIGHT LINE MAT CUTTER

1. Place a slip sheet on the base of the cutter, resting against the mat guide.

2. Set the mat guide to the desired measurement.

3. Slide the mat board, face down, under the guide rail and against the side mat guide.

4. Draw a pencil line on the matboard, against the rail. Repeat on the other three sides. Make the lines long enough to intersect at the corners.

5. Set the bevel cutter where the pencil mark intersects the guide rail, either at the top or bottom depending on whether the cutter is a push or pull style.

6. Push the blade into the board with a smooth motion, then push or pull the blade along the pencil line, stopping carefully at the point of intersection.

7. Repeat the procedure on the other three sides.

4

5

6

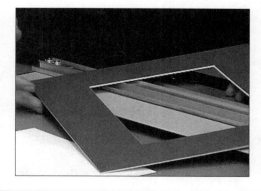

Two Methods for Cutting a Double Mat

There are two methods for cutting double mats.

METHOD ONE requires two boards of identical size, which are cut separately then joined together.

1. Cut two mat boards 11" x 14", one for the top mat, one for the undermat.

2. Set mat guides or measure and mark a 3" border on the back of the undermat board.

3. Cut all four sides of the undermat.

4. Set mat guides or measure and mark a 2-3/4" border on the back of the top mat.

5. Cut all four sides of the top mat.

6. Attach the two mats together with double-stick tape or glue. On large mats attach only along the top, to prevent future buckling from humidity.

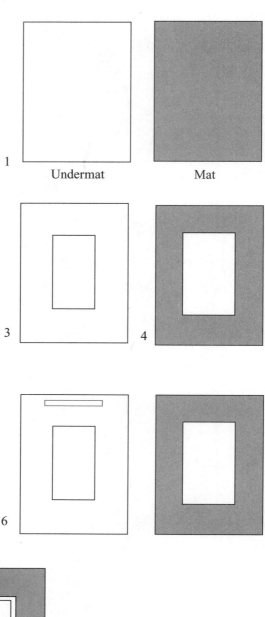

1   Undermat   Mat

3   4

6

THE PERFECT DOUBLE MAT

METHOD TWO uses a slightly smaller board for the "under-mat"—the small inner border that will show inside the window opening. The undermat is cut while attached to the top mat, allowing the top mat to serve as a template, creating identical parallel borders on both mats.

1. Cut one board 11" x 14" for top mat. Cut one board 10-3/4" x 13-3/4" for undermat. Note: The undermat board is smaller than the top mat so that its edges do not interfere with the top mat during cutting.

2. Put the board for top mat in cutter face down and cut a 2-3/4" border. Save the fallout (the rectangle of board that fell out of the opening.)

3. Apply four strips of double-sided tape to the surface of the undermat board. Attach it to the back side of the top mat.

4. Replace the fallout in the mat, attaching it to the board beneath with a short strip of double-sided tape.

5. Set mat guides or measure and mark a 3" border on the back side of the undermat board.

6. Place the boards in the mat cutter face down and cut the 3" border all the way around.

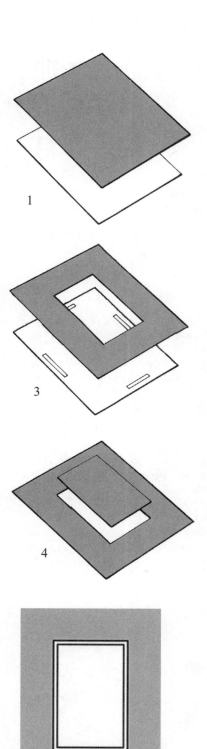

1

3

4

ADDING A V-GROOVE

V-grooves are cut into the matboard by directing bevel cuts to face each other, creating a "V" shape.
This cutting exposes the core of the board providing an accent line around the mat opening.

1. Set guide rail for a 2" border.

2. Mark a 2" border with pencil.

3. Insert the matboard *face down* into cutter and cut three sides.

4. Before cutting the fourth side, place Scotch Magic Tape over the three cuts to keep the center from dropping out.

5. Cut the fourth side.

6. Lift mat out of cutter, flip over and place back into the cutter, *face up*.

7. Do not change the 2" border setting. Insert the cutting head at the intersection of the existing cut and guide the cutter along the cut. Cut all four sides.

8. The center will drop out— tape it back in and reset the guide bar for 3".

9. Place the taped board back into the cutter *face down*. Cut the mat as usual. The center will drop out. The result is a 3" border mat with a V-groove 1" from the window opening.

V-grooves can be cut easily with a V-groove attachment that fits onto many models of Logan mat cutters.

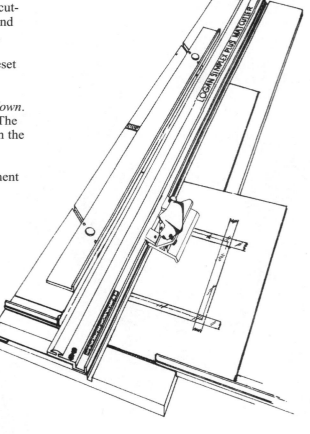

CUTTING OVAL & CIRCLE MATS

An oval opening in a window mat is an attractive way to accent art that has a centralized image. Because the corners of the artwork will be concealed, ovals can be used to minimize unwanted area around the art image. The curving line of an oval or circle has a graceful feeling, and can give an elegant character to photographs and needlework. A circle can follow the shape of a coin or other round item in the frame.

Oval and circle mats must be made with an oval and circle cutter which can cut a clean, curved line through a matboard. It is almost impossible to cut a good-looking oval or circle in a matboard with a scissors or utility knife.

When planning the border around an oval or circle opening in a rectangular mat, remember there will be lots of matting at the corners.

The oval mat cutter has two settings that together define the opening of the mat. The first is set to one dimension of the mat opening, and the other is set to the difference between the two dimensions.

For example, to make a 5"x7" opening, the first setting will be at 5", and the second will be at 2" (the difference between 5 and 7.) This will cut a 5"x7" oval in whatever size and shape of board is placed beneath the cutter.

To cut a 5" circle, the first setting will be at 5", and the second setting will be at 0" (since there is no difference between the length and width of the mat opening.)

Logan Oval & Circle Mat Cutter

CUTTING A CIRCLE MAT

The following directions are for a 10" x 10" mat with a 6" circle opening.

1. Trim a matboard to 10" x 10". Place the mat *face up* on the work surface with a scrap board, larger than the mat, as a slip sheet.

2. Adjust the cutting unit to cut a 6" circle by setting the scale arm to 6". Then set the scale inside the oval base at zero (0).

3. Push the stepping lever down until it stops. This will keep the blade from touching the board prematurely.

4. Draw four lines on the face of the mat to intersect at the precise center of the oval.

5. Place the base directly on the intersection, coordinating the markings on the base.

6. Press on the base so the base pins penetrate the matboard. Make sure the base is flat on the board.

7. Hold down the base with one hand and place right hand on scale arm with thumb on top of the adjustment block. Lift the stepping lever to the first of three positions.

8. Rotate the blade around by pulling the scale arm one quarter of the way with the right hand; rotate the matboard (and slipsheet) with the left hand and cut another quarter; rotate, cut, rotate until the blade reaches its initial point of entry.

9. Lift stepping lever to the second setting and rotate around board.

10. Lift stepping lever to the third setting and make the final revolution.

11. Before removing the base, make sure the blade has cut completely through the board. If it has not, make another revolution.

Practice! It will be easy once you have mastered the hand placement and the rotation of the matboard and slip sheet.

4

6

8

11

Decorating Mats

Most matboard surfaces will accept glue, paste, stickers, paints, rubber stamps, and inks. Items may also be attached with sewing.

The mats pictured here have been decorated in a variety of ways.

Ready-made 5"x7" frame & glass. The photo was attached with pocket corners to the backing board. A mat was cut to fit the photo into the frame. Strips of cotton eyelet were taped in position on the back of the mat.

Alphabet stickers were set on the face of the mat to add a spirit of fun to the children's mat. The frame is a ready-made 5"x7" with a mat cut to fit the photo. The photo is attached with pocket corners to the backing board.

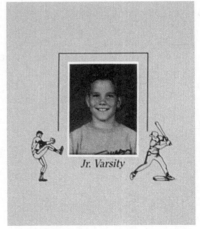

Dry transfer (rub-on) designs and rubber stamps can be used to decorate mats.

CLEANING AND CUTTING GLASS

CLEANING GLASS

Thoroughly clean the glass before laying it on the matting or artwork. If using window glass, it may be covered with a grainy resin coating that should be brushed off as much as possible before cleaning. Household glass cleaners are acceptable, but avoid ammonia and perfumes that may add unwanted chemicals to the framing package. Commercial glass cleaners are often available at hardware stores, glass shops, and craft stores that have framing departments.

CUTTING GLASS

Glass can be cut to size using a T-square and a hand-held glass cutter. The cutter typically has a rotating wheel at one end that makes a "score line" on the glass, and a ball at the other end for tapping the score to complete the cut. Logan makes a hand-held glass cutter that can be used against a T-square or in conjunction with some mat cutter bases.

1. Clean the glass before cutting for a smoother cut and to extend the life of the glass cutter. Set glass on a clean work surface; any bits of glass or wire on the work surface can scratch the glass.

2. Measure and mark where to cut the glass. Use a T-square as a guide for the cutter. Hold the glass cutter so that it rests comfortably in the hand when drawn forward. Position cutter with the wheel straight up and down, not at an angle. Use enough pressure to achieve a good score line. If white bits are being produced, the force is too great. Keep the pressure as even as possible, and run the cutter off the edge of the glass. Do not retrace the cut; it is unnecessary and can ruin the cutter. A few light or skipped spots will not affect the cut.

*Don't want to
cut glass?*

Glass and plastics can be custom cut by many craft, hobby, art supply dealers, frame shops, hardware stores, home improvement stores and glass suppliers.

This is a hand-held glass cutter. It is available with steel or carbide wheels. The ball at one end of the cutter can be used to tap on the glass to "run the score." The three notches just above the wheel can break off stray bits of glass.

3. To break the glass along the score, slide it to the edge of the work table, with the portion to be removed hanging over the edge, and snap it off. Or tap the score line with the ball end of the cutter to "run the score" and the piece will separate. There are also glass pliers available which have a special grip inside the jaws for breaking off the strip of glass.

4. If small bits of unwanted glass remain, use one of the notches on the glass cutter to remove them. Place a notch (there are typically two or three on the glass cutter) over the unwanted piece, and use the handle of the cutter as a lever to "bite" the piece off.

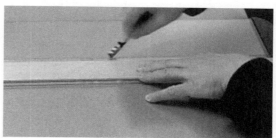

Using a T-square and glass cutter, score the glass.

CLEANING PLASTICS

Household cleaners may damage the finish of plastics, and paper towels can scratch them. Use water mixed with a tiny bit of dishwashing liquid, and apply with a soft cloth. There are special plastic cleaners that also help control static.

CUTTING PLASTIC

Use a hand-held cutter with a sharp blade. Utility knives and linoleum cutters are suitable.

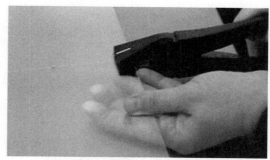

Glass pliers break the glass on the score.

1. Using a straightedge as a guide, drag the cutting blade through the plastic. Make two or three cuts until there is a groove.

2. Take the plastic to the edge of the worktable and bend it apart along the groove until it snaps.

SUPPORTING ARTWORK

All artwork put into a frame unit has to be supported. If artwork is packed in with backing, it will buckle. Some people believe that packing the frame very tightly will prevent buckles, but the reverse is true. The tighter the fit, the more it will eventually buckle and ripple.

Attachments should generally be made at the top of the art only, because artwork must be given room to expand and contract in response to changes in temperature and humidity.

Do not attach artwork on all four sides. Restriction of movement is the primary cause of buckling. Artwork must either be fully mounted or attached at the top edge.

Do not use masking tape, cellophane tape or duct tape. Even if the item is worthless, these tapes will deteriorate and leave stains.

A practical tape for holding decorative reproductions in place is Scotch Magic Tape (permanent) or Lineco's gummed Linen tape (water reversible). Be careful not to stretch the tape, or it will contract later and wrinkle the picture. Lineco's Hinging Tissue is thin but permanent and can be used to hold many types of art in place.

There are several methods for attaching artwork to its supporting board. Attaching artwork to the window mat is the easiest because it is easy to see when the artwork is centered properly in the opening. Attaching the art to the backing board takes a bit more time to center properly, but it is the preferred method because it is more supportive. The backing board is stronger because it is a solid sheet. The mat, with its window opening, is weaker; the artwork hanging from it pulls on the top of the mat, and can eventually sag. This is especially noticeable on larger pieces.

To position art correctly on the backing board, place the art on its backing, place the mat on top of the art, and adjust the artwork until it is correctly placed. Set a clean weight (such as a glass paperweight) on the art, and remove the mat. Attach the art to the backing board.

If a reproduction is under 11" x 14" and on a sturdy paper, it may be placed in the frame without support.

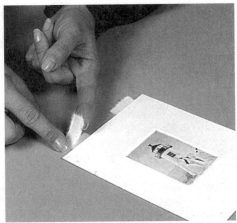

Artwork should be attached to the backing board with hinges. Here, a crosspiece is being applied to a tab hinge. The hinge is made with Japanese paper and water-reversible adhesive.

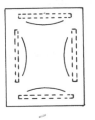
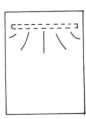

Above are examples of the results of restricting paper with tape or glue. Paper that is restricted will buckle.

HINGING PAPER ART

Pocket corners and mounting strips may be used separately or in combinations to hold artwork against the back support. It is important to allow some room for movement, or buckling will occur with changes in humidity.

Pocket corners and mounting strips are available in art supply stores, photography suppliers, or craft supply stores.

Mounting corners and mounting strips are good choices, because they make no adhesive contact at all with the art, but be sure they are made from non-acidic materials like acid-free paper or polyester material such as Mylar®.

Two pocket corners at the top and one mounting strip on the bottom. The attachment is totally reversible without using any chemicals.

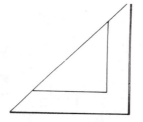

Pocket Corners are backed with pressure-sensitive adhesive; they adhere to the backing board easily.

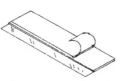

Lineco's Mounting Strips are easy to use. They attach to the backing board with a double-stick adhesive. This creates a ledge between the backing board and the clear Mylar® face.

The window mat and backing board are attached to one another along one long side. The art is hinged to the backing board.

For art that is valuable or potentially valuable (the value may be monetary or sentimental) it is wise to consider using conservation attachment methods.

Most of the methods described here can be used for conservation framing, but the choice of materials is crucial. Conservation attachments must be acid-free, and any portion that makes contact with the art must be completely reversible without damage to the art. In conservation framing, the art should be attached to a backing board made from Conservation or Museum (Rag) matboard.

The T-hinge is the most common conservation attachment. Each hinge is made from two pieces of Japanese paper. Attach about 1/8"-1/4" of one piece to the upper edge of the art paper, horizontally. Attach the rest of the hinge to the backing board by using the second piece of paper as a horizontal crosspiece. Two hinges, one placed near each top corner, is typical. Larger pieces of art may require more hinges.

Artwork may be floated by attaching a V-hinge or a pass-through hinge. The pass-through hinge involves making a slit in the backing board and slipping the hinge or tape (attached to the artwork) through it. Attach hinges or tape to the upper back side of the art, slightly below the top edge. Place the art on the backing board, and mark the placement of the hinges or tape. Make slits in the backing board where marked, then pass the hinge or tape through the slits. It is then easy to adjust the placement of the artwork. Then secure the hinge with another piece of tape to the back side of the backing board.

Conservation hinges may be made from:
1. Torn Japanese paper strips and cooked rice or wheat starch.

2. Gummed Linen or Paper tapes. See page 20.

Both are water-reversible.

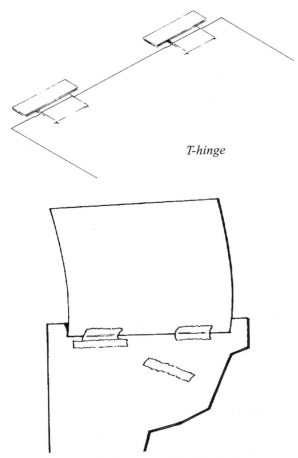

T-hinge

V-hinge for floating small works of art

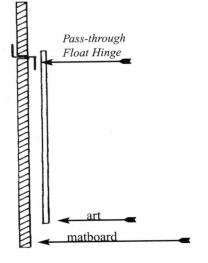

Pass-through
Float Hinge

art

matboard

MOUNTING PAPER ART

The term 'mounting' can be confusing. For framers, mounting generally refers to a full adhesion of artwork to a backing board (substrate). Full mounting completely restricts the art, so it is a very useful process for flattening and adding rigidity to decorative paper art, but it is not suitable for fine art.

Although some mounting products claim to be reversible, they are <u>not truly reversible</u>. Yes, there are ways to separate the mounted paper from the substrate, but the damage done to the item during the process, the chemicals required, and the residue that remains make this a risky and dangerous practice.

Conservation mounting is a completely different practice. Conservation methods must be totally reversible without leaving any impressions or residue (see pages 35, 36.) Conservation methods are to be used for all valuable, investment, or sentimental value pieces. Full mounting can be used for replaceable, decorative items.

There are several methods of full mounting used in frame shops, including dry (heat), wet, spray and pressure-sensitive adhesives. All mounting uses an adhesive and some form of pressure to bond the artwork to the substrate.

To be effective and maintain a pleasing appearance, the mount must be a complete attachment, not just spots or lines of glue or tape. Inadequate support will result in wrinkling, buckling, and bubbles. A successful mount is a combination of proper mounting surface, proper adhesive, and proper technique.

Not all artwork can or should be mounted. With the methods available for home use, posters, reproductions, inexpensive paper art, most photographs, and some fabrics can be mounted. Size is an important consideration. Large pieces can be very difficult to mount; problems with air bubbles, wrinkles, and tears are common. Consider using a professional framer for mounting pieces larger than 20" x 24".

Dry Mounting

Dry mounting, also called heat mounting, is a very reliable method used by professional framers and photographers. Dry mounting is fast and clean, and items properly dry mounted will stay flat and bubble-free. It requires a dry mount press (either a mechanical press or a heat vacuum press) and a heat-activated adhesive.

Reproductions with purely decorative value may be mounted to a board for a sturdy support.

FOUR FULL MOUNTING METHODS:
Dry Mounting
Wet Mounting
Pressure-Sensitive
Spray Mounting

WET MOUNTING

Wet mounting is the oldest method of permanently adhering paper or fabric to a substrate (backing board). In wet mounting, a wet paste is used in a technique similar to wallpapering. The paste is applied to the substrate, the back of the print is dampened, the two are put together, and pressure is applied until the piece is dry. Because the wet process expands the paper art to its maximum size, this mount is very strong and will stay flat.

Wallpaper paste makes a good adhesive. Since it is made to permanently hold heavy paper flat to a wall, even in high humidity, it is plenty strong enough to provide a secure mount for paper. Do not use rubber cement, or white glues.

THE PROCESS
Supplies:
• a small soft roller (2") or wide stiff brush
• paste
• scrap of glass
• clean sponge

1. Place some paste on the scrap of glass. This helps the roller pick up an even amount of paste.

2. Mist or sponge water on the back of the print; this expands the paper.

3. Apply paste to the backing board, as thinly and evenly as possible.

4. Cover the face of the print with clean paper. Set the print on the wet pasted substrate. With the face cover in place to protect the print, begin to smooth the print, starting from the middle outward using a hand or a soft rubber brayer.

5. Let dry under pressure for 6–8 hours. A piece of glass or metal plates will do.

If a mistake is made, begin to dampen slightly at the edge with a sponge and lift gently, then reapply. Be careful—wet paper tears easily.

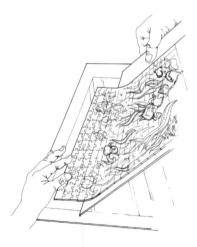

A puzzle can be wet mounted using the same directions detailed at the left. Use a sheet of matboard to transfer the puzzle to the wet backing board. Slide the puzzle onto the paste and be sure to position the puzzle squarely. Use rulers to make sure it will be square enough for the frame.

Spray Adhesives

Spray mounting is quick and inexpensive, but does not ensure a lasting bond. There are a number of spray adhesives available.

The bond is achieved by applying pressure with a roller or squeegee. Be sure to apply a thorough, even layer of adhesive. For the best bond, allow the mounted piece to dry under an even weight such as a lite of glass.

Be sure to control the spray. Wear a mask and use a ventilation fan to help reduce the fumes and the airborne particles.

Some very slick papers will resist spray adhesives, especially during times of high humidity.

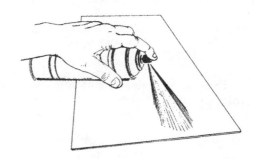

To ensure a good bond, the spray must thoroughly coat the back of the paper and the mounting board.

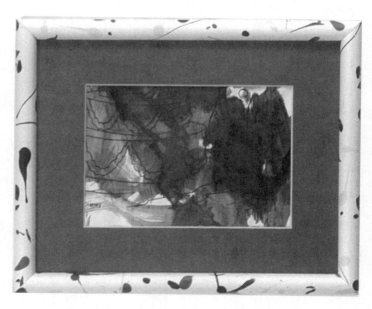

A child's painting on newsprint was mounted using spray adhesive. It was then matted and framed with a standard size single mat and frame.

Pressure-Sensitive Adhesives

Pressure-sensitive adhesive is essentially a giant piece of double-sided tape. Mounting with pressure-sensitive adhesives is sometimes called "cold mounting." These adhesives are used primarily for smaller-sized pieces no larger than 20"x24".

Mounting boards pre-coated with pressure-sensitive adhesive—often called "sticky boards"—are available in standard sizes.

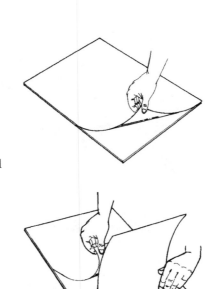

1

To mount paper using a sticky board:
1. Peel the protective sheet from the adhesive side of the board along the top edge.

2. Position the print over the board and touch the top edge of the print to the adhesive.

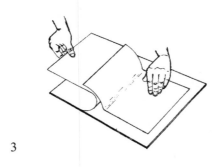

2

3. Pull off more of the protective sheet, uncovering a little adhesive at a time. Allow the print to set onto the exposed area, being careful to avoid wrinkles or creases.

4. Use a squeegee or roller to create the bond. Some adhesives are repositionable for awhile. Some require time for the bond to set. Read the instructions that come with the board.

Fabric-Covered Mats
Spray and pressure-sensitive adhesives can be used to make fabric-covered (or paper-covered) mats.

3

Following the instructions on the adhesive, apply adhesive to the back side of the fabric. Apply the fabric to the face of the already cut mat. Line up the fabric weave, and use a squeegee to secure the bond. Place the mat face down and cut out a window in the fabric, then make diagonal cuts at the corners. Wrap the fabric over the mat bevel and secure it to the back of the mat.

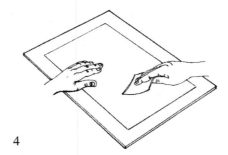

4

SHADOW BOXES

Shadow boxes are frames with enough depth to contain objects. The frame must be deep enough to hold the thickest object without letting the object touch the glass.

The next important consideration is the way the objects are attached to the backing board. Objects must be well supported. Hot glue and double-stick tape are great for crafts and decorative items, but for objects of value (whether dollar value, sentimental, or both), it is best to use an attachment method that holds securely, but leaves the objects unharmed and unaltered.

The two most common attachment methods used by professional picture framers are loops or sewn stitches of thread, cord, etc., and clear silicone adhesive.

Whenever possible, use a completely reversible method like sewing to attach items. Just a few stitches will hold most fabric items, a few loops of matching color cord can hold a golf club, and a single loop can hold an arrowhead or small figurine. Simply poke two holes in the backing board for each stitch or loop, bring the thread or cord up through one hole, through the item if it is fabric, or around an object, and back down through the second hole. Knot the ends of the thread or cord, then tape them to the back of the backing board to avoid "slump."

What about paper items that go along with the objects, like a baseball card with a baseball jersey? Use clear pocket corners (page 35) like those made for photo albums, so the card can be removed from the framing completely undamaged.

For extra interest in the shadow box design, use pocket corners to attach the card to a piece of matboard 1" larger than the card, perhaps in a contrasting color, then attach the mounted card to the backing board with double-stick tape.

Consider using hook and loop attachments (Velcro®), ribbons, cords, leather strips, buttonhole thread, etc.

A shadow box can be made from a ready-made mat and ready-made frame. The decorative dried flower is hot-glued in place.

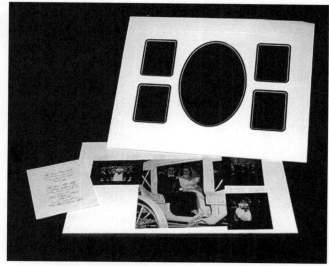

The photos and invitation are mounted onto the backing board. The mat is set over the top. The dried flower is hot-glued to the front of the mat.

THE QUICK BOX

Unlike ordinary framing, where everything hides in the rabbet of the frame, in shadow box framing some of the rabbet depth will show. To look attractive and support the backing board (to which the objects are attached), the rabbet must be lined with boards.

The lining may be created with strips of mat board, cut to the length and width of the rabbet and to the depth needed for the deepest object (plus a bit extra to provide space between the object and the glass.) Attach the strips to 1/8" foam center board. Place the frame face down. Place the glass in the frame. Glue the lining strips to the inner sides of the frame. The exposed top edge of the strips provides a ledge that serves as a rabbet. Place the backing board (with the objects attached to it) on the ledge, then fit as described in "Fitting wood frames," pages 50, 51.

QUICK BOX

This is a quick and easy trick for creating the backing and sides of the shadow box in one step.

1. Measure the rabbet size of the frame, then add the depth needed for the objects (add the depth twice, to account for both sides.). Cut the board to this size.

2. Mark the frame size on the back of the board, and score along this line on all four sides. A score is a cut that slices into, but not all the way through the board. Cut out the squares at the corners.

3. Attach the objects to the board. Fold the sides of the board upward at the score lines. Tape the outside of the corners.

FITTING A QUICK BOX

1. Lay the frame face down on a clean surface.

2. Clean the glass, and place it in the rabbet of the frame. Some framers prefer to hold the glass in the lip of the rabbet with a few dots of glue. If using glue, be sure to clean up any smears that stray beyond the lip. Place the quick box on top of the glass. Add a sheet of filler board for best support.

3. Insert nails perpendicular to the moulding to hold the box in place. See page 51.

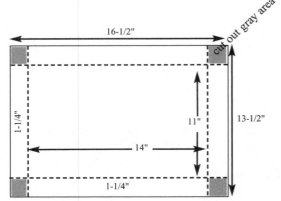

Here is a board measured for a Quick Box for an 11" x 14" frame. It is made to hold objects which are 1" thick. Note that 1-1/4" of depth is added to the frame size so the objects will not touch the glass.

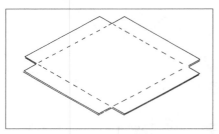

This is the same board with score lines made and the corners cut away.

Two Quick Boxes, cut and folded, ready to be taped.

When framing items of clothing, use a sheet of rag mat-board (cut to conform to the shape of the item) as a shaper. Insert the board into the shirt or dress and sew through the fabric, the shaper, and the backing board.

Acid-free tissue paper may be used to slightly pad a baby dress to give it a bit of dimension. Stitch the clothing to the backing board right through the tissue to keep it in place.

SILICONE ADHESIVE

Clear silicone adhesive (such as aquarium sealant) may be used to hold some items such as stones, glass, and metal because it has body, dries clear, and holds just about everything. There is some controversy in the picture framing industry about the use of silicone, because it releases certain gasses while drying ("curing"), and can be harmful to some items, like seashells and some metals. If using silicone adhesive, allow it to dry for a couple of days before sealing it in a frame. There is no solvent for silicone, but it can be peeled off in some cases.

HOT GLUE

There are many types of hot glue, designed to hold different types of objects and materials. Some hot glues only hold soft items such as silk flowers and fabrics. In cold weather, hot glues may become brittle and release their hold.

The seashell is held with ordinary sewing thread.

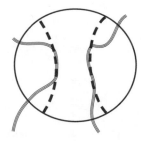

Use a crewel needle to insert quilter's thread or upholstery thread through the laces of the ball.

The little league baseball is sewn to the background. The name plate is made by printing from a computer and mounting to a piece of matboard.

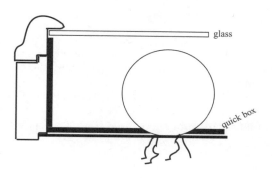

FRAMING NEEDLEWORK & FABRIC

There are many kinds of needlework, including counted cross-stitch, needlepoint, and quilting; certain principles apply to framing all of them. These principles can also be applied to framing a silk scarf and most other fabric items.

All fabrics must be supported before being framed. There are several methods used by picture framers, all of which are designed to pull the fabric taut and hold it flat. These methods are called "stretching." After stretching, the needlework can be matted and framed as desired.

Craft stores and needlework shops sell a variety of "sticky boards" (mounting board coated with a layer of pressure-sensitive adhesive) for stretching needlework. The type with adhesive on the back (but none on the face of the board) is preferable to the type with adhesive on the face. It is best if no adhesive touches the needlework, because as the adhesive ages it can damage the work and its fabric base.

The most gentle and least intrusive method for supporting fabric pieces is sewing the piece to a backing board. This is how crocheted doilies, embroidered handkerchiefs, and antique samplers are normally handled.

SEWING METHOD FOR RECTANGULAR PIECES:
Lay the needlework on the backing board it will be attached to. With a pencil, lightly mark the placement of the top edge of the needlework on the backing board. Remove the needlework. About 1/2" below the pencil mark, use an awl to poke a row of small holes, about 1" apart. Position the needlework on the backing board. Thread a needle with cotton or polyester thread. Bring the needle through the upper right hole, and through the needlework. Take a stitch about 1/4" wide, then pass the needle down through the next hole. Continue across the row of holes. Tape the loose ends of the thread to the back of the backing board.

GLASS
Some needleworks, such as needlepoints and tapestries done with wool yarns, do not need the protection of glazing, but most embroideries or cross-stitches do need glass. Be sure to use mats, or narrow matboard spacers glued to the interior sides of the frame, to raise the glazing from the surface of the needlework.

To stitch a doily (or other irregular-shaped fabric piece) to its backing board: Place the needlework on the backing board. Use an awl to poke small holes at several strategic locations (such as one at the center, and one near the tip of each "arm".) Be careful to poke through the board only, not through the needlework fibers. Use a needle and cotton or polyester thread to stitch the doily to the backing board.

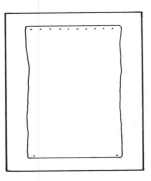

Sewing

PINNING

This is the favorite method used by professional framers for stretching cross-stitch pieces. It can also be used with silk scarves and other even-weave fabrics. This method works best with a piece of foam center board for the support, because the pins slide easily into the foam but remain firmly in place. Use stainless steel, ballpoint pins, available from most fabric stores. These pins do not pierce the fabric fibers, and will not rust.

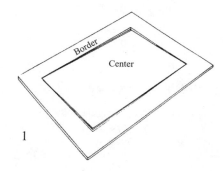

THE NEWBERRY METHOD

This method may be used alone as a stretching method, or may be used in conjunction with pinning. It provides a level surface for matting stretched needleworks.

1. Cut a piece of foam center board to the size of the frame. Cut a window (straight, not bevel) in the board slightly smaller than the mat opening. The fallout will be the support board for the needlework.

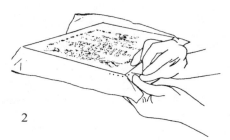

2. Center the needlework on the face of the foam center board. Guide the fabric around the sides of the board, and insert a pin into the foam core at the center of each side. Insert the pins about halfway into the foam for now.

3. Working towards the corners, place a pin about every 1/4" - 1/2". Be careful to keep the grain of the fabric straight. If necessary, remove a few pins and adjust the fabric from time to time. When satisfied with the stretch, push the pins all the way into the foam center board.

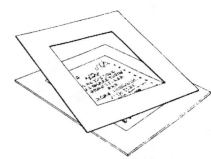

4. Insert the pinned needlework into the foam center border.

For thicker fabrics, the fallout may have to be trimmed before stretching the needlework or it may not fit back into the foam board border.

To use the Newberry Method alone for stretching, without pins, simply center the fabric on the fallout, place the foam center border over the needlework and gently press until the fallout is back in its original position. Gently pull the fabric from the back to position the piece in the center. This works great on thin fabrics.

BLOCKING A NEEDLEPOINT

BLOCKING A NEEDLEPOINT
Blocking is for needlepoint stitched with wool yarns. It allows the framer to "square-up" needlepoint canvases that have gotten stretched and distorted during the stitching process. Steam blocking avoids problems with bleeding yarns and cheap, heavily-sized canvas. It is also fast.

*Note: Some contemporary needlepoints are worked with cotton or silk yarns, and these may not require blocking before stretching. If blocking seems necessary on these pieces, test to be sure the fibers can safely tolerate heat and moisture.

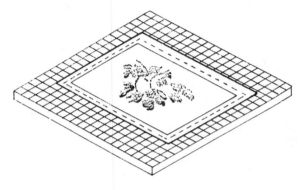

Materials:
- large wood board marked off in 1" blocks
- staple gun
- steam iron filled with distilled water

1. Line up side A and staple down (lightly).
2. Steam entire surface of needlepoint with a clean steam iron or steamer.
3. While the needlepoint is damp from the steam, pull side B to line up square and staple to the board.
4. Steam entire needlepoint again and pull side C into alignment.
5. Line up side D and steam again.
6. Measure the needlepoint while it is on the board.

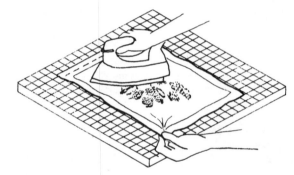

Once it has been blocked the piece can be removed and pinned, laced or stapled to matboard and then set into a frame. Wool yarn needlepoints do not need glass—in fact, wool fibers should be left exposed because they need to breathe. However, if the piece will hang in the kitchen it may be glassed for protection; the glass must be spaced away from the needlework.

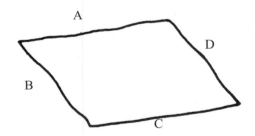

STRETCHING ON STRETCHER BARS

This is the basic method for stretching fabric on wooden stretcher bar frames. The same method is used for needlepoint, decorative fabric panels, and for paintings on canvas.

Stretcher bars are lengths of wood that interlock at the corners. They are sold as separate strips available from art supply stores. Buy two strips of the needed length size and two strips of the needed width size, and simply join the corners together. When measuring the fabric piece or painting to determine the stretcher bar size, remember to allow at least 1/2" on each of the four sides to wrap around the bars.

Materials:
Staple gun and staples
Stretcher bar frame
Canvas pliers or other broad-nosed pliers

1. Find the middle of each side of the fabric and of the stretcher bars. Mark each middle lightly with a pencil.

2. Match the pencil mark on one side of the fabric with the mark on an appropriate side of the stretcher. Bring the fabric margin to the outer edge of the bars and staple in place.

3. Go to the opposite side, and match up the pencil marks. Pull slightly to create a taut fit, then staple in place.

4. Place one staple in the center of the third side, then the fourth. There should now be a diamond-shaped taut area in the center of the fabric.

5. Begin stapling to the left and right of the center staples, working towards the corners. Do this on all sides, leaving a couple of inches free at each corner.

6. Fold the fabric neatly at each corner and staple in place.

Conservation Tip: Wooden stretcher bars are acidic. If the needlework or other fabric being stretched is valuable, either seal the bars with an acrylic wood sealer, or glue a sheet of rag matboard to the face of the bars before stretching.

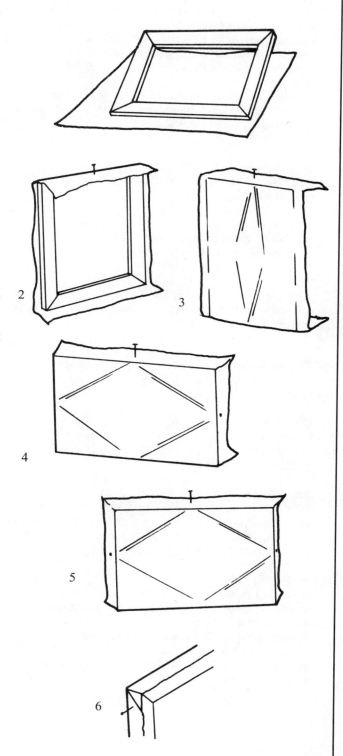

FITTING

The term "fitting" is used by professional framers to refer to the process of assembling all of the items that will go into the frame, installing them in the frame, sealing up the back, and attaching the hardware for hanging. Here is an overview of the materials needed for fitting.

Hammers: A small claw hammer, tack hammer or other, but make sure it has a small head, to minimize the force and tap easily against the heads of small nails.

Nails
Short, thin, sharp wire brads to nail sideways into the rabbet of the frame. Hard woods like oak and maple will require pre-drilling.

Screwdrivers
For joining metal frames, depending on the hardware. Have several sizes handy.

Drill
This may be needed for pre-drilling the holes for nails and screw eyes in very hard woods. Small bits, proportionate to the nails, will be needed.

Dusting Brush
Extremely useful for removing dust and other particles from the glass, mat, and artwork before sealing up the frame.

Glass Cleaner
Choose one with no ammonia, coloring or perfume, to minimize the chemical residue that will be sealed into the framing.

Paper Towels
For cleaning the glass and frame. Plain white or brown kraft is best, so there is no chance of color transfer to artwork, matting, or other parts of the framing. Fluffy towels leave more lint than hard commercial towels.

Measuring Ruler
Measuring of frames and all other framing materials should be done with a good quality carpenter's rule, artist's rule or metal tape measure. Yardsticks and cloth measuring tapes are not accurate enough for framing purposes. Even 1/8" of incorrect measurement could result in buckled artwork, so using a good measuring device is very worthwhile.

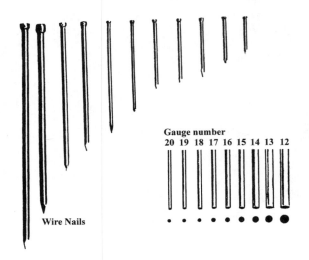

Wire brads are thin and can be used to join corners of frames together, as well as to hold the framing package in the frame.

A genuine hair dusting brush will help reduce dust particles when fitting the framing package together.

Dust Cover Paper
A sheet of paper large enough to cover the entire back of the frame, typically brown or black kraft paper such as that used for mailing or wrapping packages. If framing valuable art, use sheets of good quality artist sketch paper.

White Glue or Double-stick Tape
This is used to attach the backing paper to the back of the frame.

Cutting Blade
Single-edge razor blade or utility knife for trimming the backing paper flush with the edges of the frame.

Hanging Hardware
Attaches to the back of the frame to allow hanging on the wall. Screw eyes, sawtooth hangers, or D-rings can all be used. All are available at craft, hardware, and home improvement stores. Use a size appropriate for the size and weight of the frame.

Braided Wire
If using screw eyes, wire will be wound around the eyes. Choose a wire with a breaking point about 3 times the weight of the picture.

Choose a screw eye that is proportionate to the size of the moulding and the weight it must support.

D-rings or mirror hangers can be screwed into the wood frame. They may be used with or without wire.

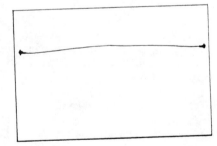

Attach the wire about one-third to one-fourth of the way down from the top edge of the frame, leaving a little slack so the wire can be set onto a nail or hanger.

FITTING WOOD FRAMES

Fitting involves assembling and cleaning all of the items that will go into the frame, installing the entire package in the frame, and finishing the back, typically with a dust cover and hanging hardware.

During this process, it is important to avoid using too much pressure, which could cause buckling of the artwork, matting, and backing boards in the future.

THE SANDWICH FIT

The "sandwich fit" is a very useful fitting technique that keeps all of the materials clean and dust-free during the fitting process, and provides a moisture and pollution barrier for the artwork.

1. Stack the backing board, artwork, mats, and thoroughly cleaned glass face up on the worktable.

2. Using 3/4"-wide Scotch Magic Tape, place a continuous strip of tape along one side of the stack. Attach 1/8" of the tape to the surface of the glass, then wrap the rest around the sides of the stack and attach it to the back side of the backing board.

3. Continue on the other three sides of the stack, creating a u-channel that encases all of the materials in the stack.

A NOTE ABOUT SPACERS

It is generally best to keep the glazing away from the surface of artwork. Matting is the most common spacer, but sometimes a framer does not want a mat on the art. Other materials, such as narrow balsawood strips or matboard strips, can be used to separate the glazing from the surface of the artwork. After placing the glass or plastic in the frame, glue 1/8" strips of spacer to the inner sides of the frame, resting against the glass. Then proceed with the fitting as described in this section. The spacers will be hidden by the lip of the frame rabbet.

This is the basic procedure for fitting a wood frame. If the wood is very hard, drill holes before inserting nails or screw eyes.

1. Assemble the materials on a clean work surface. For art on paper, this will be glazing, art, matting or spacers, and backing board.

2. Clean the glass. Brush dust and lint off the art, mats, and backing board. Stack the layers in order. If desired, tape together in the sandwich fit method.

3. Place the frame face down. Insert the stack face down in the rabbet of the frame. If the frame is larger than 8" x 10", add an additional "filler" board for support. Use the same material as the backing board.

4. Set a nail on the back with the point against the frame. Tap the nail head with a hammer, guiding it straight into the wood. Do not allow the nail to angle downward, as this places too much pressure on the art and other boards. Install another nail about 2" away from the first; continue all the way around the frame.

5. Apply glue or double-sided tape to the back edges of the frame. Avoid getting glue on the sides of the frame, as it can damage the finish.

6. Place the dustcover paper on the adhesive. Pull and smooth as needed to make the paper taut.

7. Using a single-edged razor blade or a utility knife, trim the paper flush with the edges of the frame. Hold the blade at an angle for a clean cut. Some framers trim the paper about 1/8" from the edge, guiding the blade across the back of the frame with a ruler.

8. Use an awl to poke two holes, one on the left side of the back of the frame, one on the right, to hold the screw eyes. Place the holes about 1/3 of the way down from the top of the frame. Insert the screw eyes, and use the awl to twist them into the frame.

9. Insert one end of the wire into one of the screw eyes. Wrap it around and bring it through the eye a second time. Wrap the excess wire neatly for an inch or two, then cut the rest off. Extend the wire to the other screw eye, allowing some slack—do not pull the wire taut—and repeat the wrapping procedure.

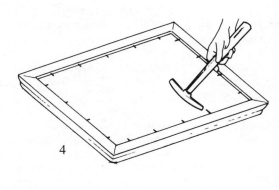

4

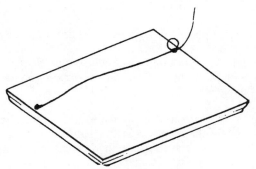

FITTING METAL FRAMES

Sectional metal frames are easy to put together. Different companies provide slightly different hardware, but most of them work the same way.

1. Prepare a clean work surface. Wood splinters and bits of glass can scratch the frame. Lay out the frame sections face down.

2. Insert one of the L-shaped hardware pieces (some brands require two pieces) into both ends of one frame section. Slide the two adjoining sections onto the hardware, and tighten the screws. Adjust the alignment of the frame sections during tightening if necessary, to make the corners join neatly.

3. Stack the glass, mats, artwork and backing together, and slide this unit into the channel of the frame. The layers can be inserted separately, but be careful not to scratch the surface of the mats or artwork on the edge of the glass.

4. Insert the remaining angle hardware into the remaining section of the frame. Slide the hardware into the side pieces of the frame, and tighten the screws. Once again, check the alignment of the corners while tightening, or tighten, check, loosen and adjust as needed.

5. There may be space remaining in the frame channel. The space must be filled in some way to hold the materials securely in the frame. The packet of hardware may have included "spring clips," which can be inserted between the frame rail and the backing board. These can place too much pressure on the materials in the frame, resulting in buckling of mats or artwork in the future. To avoid this, use strips of matboard or foam center board instead of the clips, or open one end of the frame and add additional full sheets of backing board. (Not too tight—the fit should be secure but should not exert pressure.)

6. Insert the hanging hardware provided with the frame, which may be one sawtooth hanger or two pieces with holes for attaching wire.

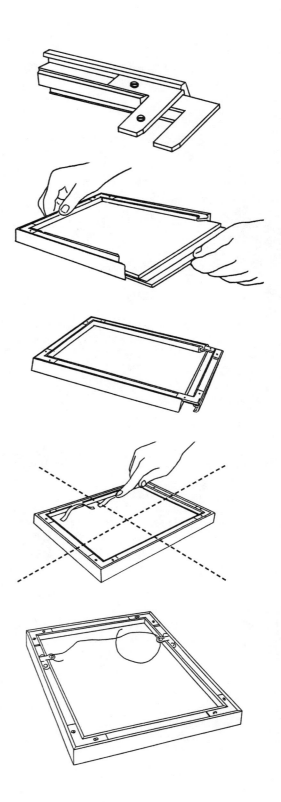

FITTING ART ON CANVAS

Art on canvas may be an original oil or acrylic painting, a photograph or print mounted on canvas, or an image printed directly on canvas fabric. Art on canvas is light in weight, so frames do not have to be exceptionally strong to hold them, even for large pieces.

Since most art on canvas is stretched on wooden stretcher bars, which are thick (often 3/4"), the depth of the frame rabbet is an important consideration. It is best if the stretcher bars rest fully within the rabbet, but often this is not possible, because most frames simply aren't that deep. If the stretcher bars will extend out the back of the frame, a wider style of moulding (such as 2" wide) looks much better than a narrow moulding when hanging on the wall.

Oil and acrylic paintings should be framed without glass or any other type of cover sheet. They are left exposed to the air, which is best for the paint, and allows viewers to enjoy the texture and brushstrokes of the painting. Photos and prints on canvas are designed to emulate oil paintings, so their surfaces generally have a protective surface that does not need to be glassed.

To fit canvas artwork into a frame:
1. Lay the frame face down on a clean surface.

2. Place the canvas face down in the rabbet.

3. If the canvas fits entirely into the rabbet, fit as with paper art, tapping nails sideways into the frame. The nails should hold the canvas with gentle pressure, not pressing it down tightly. If the canvas sticks out of the frame, use offset clips or any sort of hardware that functions similarly (screws into the frame, holds the canvas without puncturing the bars.) Toe nailing is the least preferred method because it makes holes in the stretcher bars.

4. Attach a dust cover to the back of the frame, then add hanging hardware: either screw eyes and wire, or D-rings without wire for large, heavy frames.

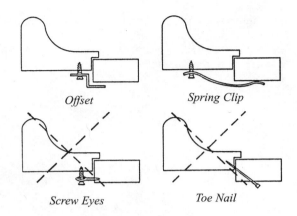

Offset *Spring Clip*

Screw Eyes *Toe Nail*

Four clips (one placed near each corner) will give the best support while still allowing freedom of movement for the canvas and stretcher bars. An additional clip may be added to each of the long sides of larger pieces.

Use D-rings without wire on very large or heavy frames, to keep the piece close to the wall and manage the stress on the frame.

TIPS FOR FRAMING

The suggestions here are guidelines for handling different types of artwork. Some use practical framing methods, which are intended for use with decorative art. Others use conservation framing methods, which are intended for valuable art (whether sentimental value or dollar value.) Remember to consider the current and potential future value of the art, and the importance of preserving it, when making framing decisions.

ART ON PAPER

Prints, drawings, watercolors, photographs—any art done on paper should be matted and glassed. Although it may seem simpler to place the artwork directly against the glass and seal up the frame, it is not a healthy practice for artwork. When artwork is pressed against the glass, condensation may form within the frame, causing buckling and staining, promoting the growth of mold, or the work may even stick to the glass. Even if the artwork is mounted for stiffness or has been done on a stiff board that will not buckle, it should be spaced away from the glazing with spacers or matting.

The white border on a reproduction is a "carrier sheet" for handling purposes—it is not meant to show. When matting a reproduction, the mat opening should cover all the carrier sheet and come slightly over the edge of the image.

FINE ART PRINTS

FINE ART PRINTS, also called Original Prints, may be made one-at-a-time by an artist (silkscreens, for example) or may be printed in pre-determined quantities (limited edition.) These prints are signed by the artist (and are often numbered), usually in pencil. Mat openings for these prints usually start 1/4" away from the edge of the image or plate mark. More space may be allowed to accommodate the signature. Never cut the carrier sheet (the extra paper surrounding the print) of a valuable print. The collector value of the piece may be reduced or even cancelled by alteration of the original sheet.

REPRODUCTIONS • POSTERS • DIPLOMAS • PRINT-OUTS

REPRODUCTIONS AND POSTERS
The printed information on a poster is often part of the design and should be matted and or framed to show it in its entirety.

If the poster is strictly for decorative purposes the words may be cut off or covered with a mat. If it has value it should not be altered in any way.

Be careful with surface finishes on posters. Some scratch easily and repel adhesives. Attempts to erase marks on posters can ruin the surface. Always test in an obscure corner.

Most posters can be mounted with wet, spray or pressure-sensitive mounting methods, or in the dry mount press. Although many people like to fully mount a poster then put it into the frame without a spacer or mat—be careful—the poster may stick to the glass.

CERTIFICATES AND DOCUMENTS
These should be handled relative to their worth. Ordinary paper certificates can be fully mounted.

University degrees and diplomas should be treated like valuable pieces of artwork. Provide a glass and mat with conservation methods and materials.

Do not laminate important documents—the lamination will never be removed and will discolor over time.

COMPUTER PRINTING PROCESSES
Computer technologies have made possible a wide variety of printing processes, and new ones are constantly created. People can make color photocopies, print photos on do-it-yourself printers at the drug store, and use home printers to print on all sorts of paper, even plastic, using all sorts of inks. All of these may be problematic. They may smear if exposed to moisture, and fade if exposed to too much light. They may be heat-sensitive and turn black or discolor.

In short, before attempting any mounting process, other than pocket corners, test a corner of the item. UV filtering glass can help slow the fading.

CHILDREN'S ART • WATERCOLORS

Children's art is often done on construction paper or newsprint, and both of these papers can fade quickly and become brittle. Framing can help preserve them. Use mats and glass on kid's art.

If there are objects attached, such as leaves or pieces of scrap material, take a moment to glue them down—library paste doesn't hold any better now than it did when you were a kid!

Up The Water Spout

The spider on the waterspout and the straw must be spaced from the glass. Use spacers under the mat to lift the mat up. This will create a nice-looking shadow, adding depth to the framing. Attach the art to the backing board with tape or hinges at the top edge.

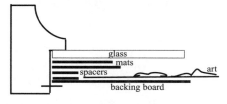

BUCKLED WATERCOLORS

Because wetness wrinkles paper, it is the nature of watercolors to be buckled. To diminish the look of buckling and keep the watercolor from touching the glass use a double mat and a spacer. Lift the mat from the backing board with two layers of matboard—use strips of matboard attached to the backing board with white glue or double-stick tape. Do not attach the strips to the watercolor paper. The watercolor should be attached to the backing board with hinges. Then set the mat on the spacer strips. The depth will accommodate the buckles.

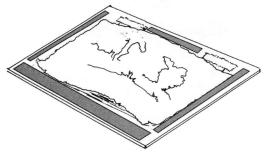

Attach narrow strips of matboard around the edges of the watercolor paper. Leave a bit of space for the watercolor to expand during times of high humidity.

POSTCARDS

A great selection of miniature art images is available in the form of postcards, sold in bookstores, catalogues and museum gift shops—or perhaps you've bought some while traveling.

"Floating" artwork on a background color gives added dimension, and avoids the need for a mat with exactly the right opening. Here are two different uses for a frame.

Directions for single image version:
1. Attach a strip of double-sided tape (about three inches long) along top back edge of postcard.
2. Position card on matboard and press to adhere.

Here a single image is "floated" in the mat opening. Notice that the art is positioned in a balanced but not exactly equal proportion.

The set of four art postcards make a nice vertical grouping in ready-made 5" x 7" frames. The deckled edges on the cards add dimension.

Directions:
1. Trim all edges of the cards with deckle scissors (Fiskars Paper Edgers ® Scissors, Deckle style.)

2. Attach a strip of double-sided tape (about two inches long) along the top back edge of each postcard.

3. Center each card on a 5" x 7" piece of matboard. When properly positioned, press to adhere.

These postcards were trimmed a bit to fit into two ready-made 4"x6" frames. Add a piece of backing and a hanger. No glass required.

Pen & Ink • Drawings • Newsprint

Watercolors/Pen & Ink Drawings

These are both wet art mediums usually done on rather soft paper. The paper may be wavy and buckled from the application of wet paint or ink. Do not fully mount original watercolors or drawings. Leave the wrinkles as they are.

These works should be matted to keep the surface from touching the glazing. The mat on a watercolor painting usually rests on the edge of where the paint stops, or the mat may overlap some of the paint. Pen and ink drawings are generally centered on the paper, so the mat area is negotiable.

Use conservation boards and attachments for valuable works, and UV-filtering glass.

Charcoals, Soft Pastels, & Pencil Drawings

• The delicate surface requires matting and glass.
• Do not use acrylic sheeting or any type of plastic glazing. Static will transfer loose particles from the artwork image onto the plastic.
• Avoid using spray fixatives; most will eventually discolor and they are not removable.
• If the pastel work is heavy, there will be lots of loose particles. A raised mat can be made by attaching strips of matboard or foam center board to the underside of the window mat. The pastel is then attached to the backboard. Loose chalk particles will fall into the gap. Heavy pastel work is difficult to handle—do not shake it! Be careful to avoid excessive jarring when inserting fitting hardware in the frame.
• Use conservation boards and attachments, and UV-filtering glass.

Newspaper Clippings

Newsprint yellows and becomes brittle. Here are several ways to handle newsprint.

• Make a photocopy on good paper and frame the copy.
• Put the original in a see-through envelope used by stamp collectors; then frame the envelope.
• Spray glue or double-stick pressure-sensitive adhesive (see page 40) can be used to mount the clipping to a dark gray or black matboard. The dark matboard prevents the printing on the reverse side from being seen through the thin paper.
• The clipping will last longer if treated with with a deacidification spray such as Archival Mist® to neutralize the acids in the newsprint. The clipping will eventually yellow, but will not become brittle.

PHOTOGRAPHS

PHOTOGRAPHS

Most photos should be matted and glassed to protect their surface. If pressed against the glass without a mat or spacer, photos will stick to the glass. Some photos are mounted to a fabric and stretched over wooden stretcher bars, and are brush-stroked to simulate an oil painting. These can be put into a frame without glass like an oil painting (page 53).

This sepia photo was fully mounted with a sheet of pressure-sensitive film to a sheet of matboard, then matted using the same color.

This photograph is held with gummed paper hinges to the backing board, then double matted, glassed and framed with a matching color metal section frame.

MEMORY BOOK pages typically come in two sizes: 8-1/2"x11" and 14"x14". Because the page often has several layers pasted to it, the page must be matted to keep it away from the glass. Use either a double mat or put a layer of matboard pieces under the mat to lift it off of the page. This is especially important for glossy photos which often stick to the glass.

The page at the right is a 14"x14" with a one-inch mat making the frame a 16"x16". The frame was made from two sets of 16" wood sections. Section frames are explained on page 8.

COMPETITION PHOTOGRAPH

This 8" x 10" photo has been mounted to a sheet of art paper; the art paper is mounted to a 16" x 20" black competition mounting board.

1. Apply pressure-sensitive film to the back side of the photo. Burnish in place.

2. Apply pressure-sensitive film to the back side of the art paper. Burnish in place.

3. Trim the edges of the photograph to the exact size required, with an X-Acto® knife and T-square.

4. Peel off the back of the sticky film and mount the photo onto the art paper.

5. Trim the art paper (with the photo mounted on it) to exact size required.

6. Measure for exact placement on the mount board and peel the release paper off the back of the art paper and mount to the board.

PHOTO FRAMES
Photographs placed into frames without mats are in danger of sticking to the glass. A narrow piece of matboard can be place under the edge of the lip of the frame between the glass and the photo to keep the photo from touching the glass. Some photos can be sprayed with a photographer's spray to keep the surface from sticking to the glass.

Narrow spacers of matboard have been placed between the glass and the photos.

Photo Collage

Snapshots can be assembled into a collage on a sticky board, then matted.

1. Cut the sticky board to the outer size of the mat.

2. Peel off the cover sheet, exposing the sticky surface.

3. Trim the photos before stetting them next to each other to get the best of the snapshot. Arrange the photos (careful, they may stick quick!)

4. After all snapshots have been positioned, set the cover sheet on top of the photos and burnish using a roller.

5. Remove the cover sheet and set the mat on the sticky surface.

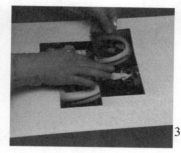

2   3

Needlework

Cross-Stitch and needlepoint may be framed without glass. If the piece has beads or embellishments that rise above the fabric, a spacer will be necessary if the needlework is to be covered with glass.

Matting a Needlework

When using a mat on needlework, add spacers under the mat to compensate for the thickness of the fabric. Use layers of matboard to create the necessary amount of depth. Attach the spacing with double-sided tape at the outer edges of the mat. The thicker the fabric to be matted the more spacing needed. The Newberry method of stretching (page 45) makes it easy to mat needlework.

• Needlepoint and crewel work made with wool yarns should not be glassed. It seals the natural fibers from necessary air circulation, causing mildew and rot.

• Glazing is optional on most fabric pieces. If glazing is used, always add some sort of spacer to keep the fabric from touching the glazing.

This fine embroidery has beads worked into the stitches. The mats keep the beads from touching the glass.

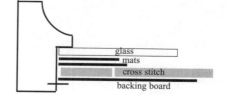

PAINTINGS ON CANVAS

- Usually done with oil or acrylic paints, but may be wax-based or other media.
- Canvas is cotton or linen. The canvas is stretched over wooden stretcher bars or mounted on cardboard panels.
- Some artists paint on Masonite or other hardboards.
- Paintings on canvas are framed without glass to provide ample air circulation. Deterioration of the canvas and paint will eventually result if sealed under glass. Museums may glass oil and acrylic paintings to protect them from being touched while on display. Not only are spacers provided between glass and painting, the frames are frequently opened to check the paintings and give them air.
- Liners are used instead of matting to provide a border around paintings on canvas. Most liners are made of wood, between 1/2" and 4" wide, covered with white or cream linen or other fabric. A narrow wooden lip called a "fillet" may be used to accent the inside edge of the liner.
- Frames for paintings on canvas may be a wide variety of styles and sizes—from narrow, deep, contemporary styles, to wide, ornate gold period frames—depending on the character of the painting and the decor it will hang with.

See page 53 for information about fitting paintings on canvas into frames.

See page 47 "Stretching on Stretcher Bars".

The size and style of the frame moulding should complement the painting style.

A small painting on a canvas panel fits nicely into a ready-made 5"x7" frame.

A simple wood frame suits this child's painting on canvas.

PRODUCT LIST

Logan Mat Cutters

Model#   Description

#1100

Hand-Held Mat Cutters

1100   **Basic** Push Style mat cutter with fixed blade.

2000   **Advanced** Push style mat cutter with retractable blade.

3000   **Pro-Am** Pivot & Pull style mat cutter with pivoting blade.

4000   **Original** Pivot & Pull style mat cutter with pivoting blade and marker bar.

701   **Straight Cutter** with three depth settings. Adapts onto many Logan mat cutters.

704   **Glass Cutter** with hardened steel wheel. Adapts onto many Logan mat cutters.

1500   **Foamboard Cutter** cuts 45 & 90 degrees. Can be used against any suitable straight-edge.

#2000

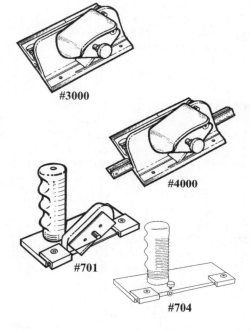

#3000

#4000

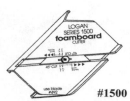

#1500

Team Systems

424   **Team System** 24" ruled aluminum guide rail with 2000 mat cutter.

440   **Team System** 40" ruled aluminum guide rail with 3000 mat cutter.

441   **Team System** 40" ruled aluminum guide rail with 4000 mat cutter.

#701

#704

#424

Board Mounted Mat Cutters

250   **Craft & Hobby Cutter** 24" base board with guide rail, squaring bars and model 500 mat knife.

301   **Compact** 32" base board with guide rail, mat guide and bevel cutting head.

301-S   **Compact** 32" base board with guide rail, mat guide, bevel cutting head and straight cutting head.

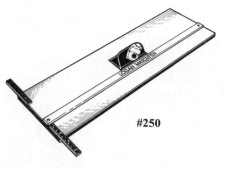

#250

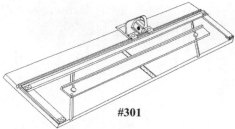

#301

Logan Mat Cutters

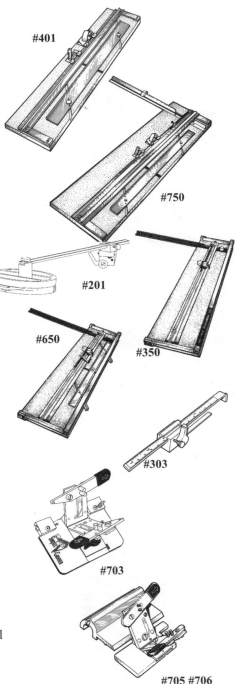

Model#	Description

401   ***Intermediate*** 40" base board with guide rail, mat guide, squaring bar, bevel cutting head and straight cutting head.

750   ***SimplexPlus*** 40" base board with guide rail, mat guide in aluminum channels, 27" squaring arm, two guide rail stops, durable laminate surface, bevel cutting head and straight cutting head.

Oval & Circle Mat Cutter

201   ***3-Step Oval & Circle*** Mat Cutter includes practice matboard and 6 blades. Cuts oval from 3-1/4" x 4-3/4" to 20" x 23". Circles from 4" to 20".

Professional Production Mat Cutters

350   ***Designer's Edge*** 40" base board with dual purpose straight and bevel cutting head, 27" squaring arm and production stops.

650   ***Framer's Edge*** 40" base board with dual purpose straight and bevel cutting head, 27" squaring arm, laminated top, mat guide and production stops.

Surface V-Groovers

703   ***Simplex V-Groover*** cuts beautiful V-Grooves on the surface of the matboard. Includes stop. Operates on any #700 Simplex. Operates on #301 Compact or #401 Intermediate with the use of the ***#303 Compact V-Groove Adapter.***

705   ***Logan V-Groover*** cuts beautiful V-Grooves on the surface of the matboard. Includes stop. Operates on any Logan Professional Production Mat Cutter including models: #310, #350, #600, #650 & #660.

706   ***Logan Universal V-Groover*** cuts beautiful V-Grooves on the surface of the matboard. Includes two stops. Operates on any professional mat cutter with a 5/8" thick rod on the cutting bar.

Logan Graphic Products, Inc.
1100 Brown Street Wauconda, IL 60084
847-526-5515 Toll Free 1-800-331-6232

See us at **www.logangraphic.com**
E-MAIL cs@logangraphic.com